101 Itty Bitty Celebrations

2" WOOL STITCHERIES TO MAKE AND SHARE

Lisa Bongean of Primitive Gatherings

Martingale®
Create with Confidence

101 Itty Bitty Celebrations:
2" Wool Stitcheries to Make and Share
© 2021 by Lisa Bongean

Martingale®
18939 120th Ave. NE, Ste. 101
Bothell, WA 98011-9511 USA
ShopMartingale.com

Printed in Hong Kong
26 25 24 23 22 21   8 7 6 5 4 3 2 1

Library of Congress Cataloging-in-Publication Data
is available upon request.

ISBN: 978-1-68356-115-6

MISSION STATEMENT

We empower makers who use fabric and yarn
to make life more enjoyable.

CREDITS

PUBLISHER AND
CHIEF VISIONARY OFFICER
Jennifer Erbe Keltner

CONTENT DIRECTOR
Karen Costello Soltys

DESIGN MANAGER
Adrienne Smitke

MANAGING EDITOR
Tina Cook

PRODUCTION MANAGER
Regina Girard

ACQUISITIONS AND
DEVELOPMENT EDITOR
Laurie Baker

COVER AND
BOOK DESIGNER
Kathy Kotomaimoce

COPY EDITOR
Sheila Chapman Ryan

PHOTOGRAPHERS
Adam Albright
Brent Kane

ILLUSTRATOR
Teri Heenan

contents

introduction

Every day is a gift, so let's celebrate with these little wool appliquéd and embroidered Itty Bitties! Measuring in at a whopping 2" to 2⅛" square, they are the perfect way to enjoy a little dose of all the things you love and get a quick appliqué fix at the same time. Do you have a favorite holiday? There's at least one design for all the major ones and even some not-so major ones. (Is Groundhog Day a major holiday? Doesn't matter; there's an Itty Bitty for it.) What about sports, you ask? Yep, got most of them covered too. Seasons? Uh huh, they're all included. Pets? Of course.

Basically, there's something for just about everyone. With 101 designs to choose from, you're going to find a lot to stitch. I guarantee it. They're kind of like potato chips; once you get started, it's hard to stop. And you need a different one for every week, right? Actually, if you stitched them all, you'd have almost enough to change out the design twice a week (or display two at a time) for an entire year.

So, what do you do with these little guys once you've stitched up one or a gazillion? Pretty much anything. My favorite way to display them is on a little wood clipboard that I carry in my shops (PrimitiveGatherings.us). They come in black and white, so all the Itty Bitties look great on them, as you can see in some of the photos where the clipboards were used. You could also hang them on your bulletin board, put a pin back on them and wear them, tuck them into a vignette, or mail one to a friend just because. These are fun projects, so have fun displaying them!

OK, enough talking. Grab your bits and pieces of wool (these are great for those small scraps you've been saving!), your balls and skeins of pearl cotton and floss, and get to it. There are Itty Bitties waiting to be stitched!

~Lisa

Happy Is the New Pretty
(page 13)

5

itty bitty supplies

Itty Bitties are made by either appliquéing wool shapes onto a wool base or by embroidering on wool. If you've done wool appliqué before, you've probably got everything you need (which isn't much!). Here's what you should have on hand.

FELTED WOOL

Itty Bitties don't require much fabric (they finish at roughly 2" square), so they're ideal for using your wool scraps. Make sure you're using wool that has already been felted so the edges of the appliquéd shapes and the background squares won't ravel.

Wool can be purchased already felted, or you can buy unfelted wool and felt it yourself. I like to use 100% wool fabrics. When felted, it creates a dense fabric with a fuzzy texture.

DOUBLE-SIDED FUSIBLE WEB

Using a double-sided fusible allows you the option of temporarily sticking the shapes to the background piece, moving them around as you need to, and then fusing them in place when you're ready. I also like the clean edge fusible web gives to the shapes; using fusible controls the fuzziness of the wool at the edges by keeping the fibers in place.

HeatnBond Feather Lite is my favorite double-sided fusible web because it bonds securely. Other brands lack the stickiness needed to keep the shapes in place until they're stitched down. There's nothing more aggravating than having a piece pop off the background while I'm stitching, or even worse, having a piece go missing!

The key to a good bond is the STEAM. Lite Steam-A-Seam 2 needs a generous amount of steam. Don't be timid! You can't wreck a piece of felted wool with steam. Once the shapes are properly fused in place (this is explained beginning on page 9), they're not going anywhere . . . but you can. There's no need to worry about losing an appliqué shape, so Itty Bitties are perfect for taking-along projects. Take several; they stitch up quick! Even if you're making an Itty Bitty that doesn't have appliqué, the front and back wool squares are fused together, so you'll need fusible for all your projects.

MARKING TOOLS

I keep an assortment of marking tools on hand for different tasks.

Sharpie. I like to use an ultra-fine-point Sharpie to trace patterns onto fusible web and to trace words onto Glad Press'n Seal (more on that later).

Clover white marking pen. This pen is good for marking any lines that will be stitched on medium- and dark-colored wools. Use a light touch when marking with this pen; the mark doesn't show up immediately, but the liquid gets darker as it dries. Remove the marks with steam.

FriXion pen. Use this pen for marking lines that will be stitched on light-colored wool. Marks can be erased with heat, but they come back when exposed to extreme cold, so make sure any marks you make will be stitched over.

THREADS

I typically use four weights of thread when stitching Itty Bitties: size 5 pearl cotton, size 8 pearl cotton, size 12 pearl cotton, and three-strand floss (which can be separated). The larger the number, the finer the thread.

I prefer using hand-dyed Valdani pearl cotton and floss in my work. Each project will indicate the weight and the color number of the thread I used.

NEEDLES

I primarily use size 22 and 24 chenille needles from my company, Primitive Gatherings, for stitching on wool. The needles are sharper and shorter than other brands, making them easier to work with.

PRESSING TOOLS

A good steam iron with a wool setting is essential to properly adhere the fusible web to the wool fibers. The more steam the iron produces, the better. I do a lot of fusible-wool appliqué, so my iron of choice is the Rowenta Perfect Steam Station. You can make a lot of Itty Bitties before you have to refill the tank!

A 100% wool pressing mat is another great tool to have. The mat holds the heat and steam from the iron and pushes it back up into the piece, essentially pressing it from both sides at once to create a firm bond.

CUTTING TOOLS, RULERS, AND TWEEZERS

A good pair of scissors is essential when cutting through the thickness of wool, so invest in a 5" to 6" pair for this task. Make sure the scissors feel good in your hand and have comfortable finger holes, as well as a smooth cutting action.

Cutting the front and back squares for the Itty Bitties is easiest done with a rotary cutter, mat, and acrylic ruler.

Fine-tipped tweezers are helpful for removing fusible-web paper from the back of appliqués and for placing appliqués on the front square.

GLAD PRESS'N SEAL

When you need to transfer words and designs that will be embroidered onto wool or dark fabrics that you can't see through, reach for Glad Press'n Seal plastic wrap. You can find this product in most grocery stores in the aisle with other plastic wraps and foil.

From left to right: House (page 43), Birthday Cake (page 47), and Reindeer (page 63)

how to make an itty bitty

Itty Bitties are meant to be fun. Use whatever fabric colors you want to use, or refer to the project photo to use something similar to what I selected for my Itty Bitties. Do what makes you happy! Stitches and thread colors to use are given in the instructions, but you'll need to refer to the photos for the detail lines. I usually freehand most of the detail stitching, but if it makes you feel better, use one of the marking tools I mentioned on page 7 and mark the lines. Just don't get stressed about it! A photo tutorial of my appliqué process can be found in my book *Wool, Needle & Thread* if you need additional information on the techniques I use.

1   From the wool for the front and back, cut two squares, 2¼" × 2¼".

2   Trace a 2¼" square and all of the project's appliqué shapes onto the paper side of the fusible web using an ultra-fine-tip Sharpie. (Patterns have already been reversed for the fusible-web technique.) If your pattern has words and/or an embroidered design, trace the words and/or design onto the non-sticky side of a piece of Glad Press'n Seal, in addition to tracing the 2¼" square onto the fusible web. Roughly cut out each appliqué shape, including the 2¼" square. (If your Itty Bitty is all embroidered, you can skip steps 3–9).

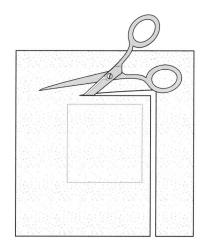

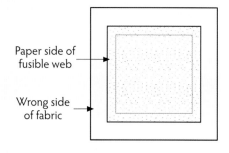

3 Carefully peel off the paper backing from each shape to expose the tacky side of the fusible web. Make sure the fusible layer stays with the gridded paper side you traced on. Position each fusible-web shape on the appropriate wool piece, positioning the 2¼" square on the wrong side of the backing square. Do NOT press yet!

4 With a *dry* iron (do not use steam on paper), press each shape. The fusible-web paper will have a grayish cast once it adheres to the wool; this is normal, so don't be alarmed.

5 Cut out all the fusible shapes, except for the backing square, cutting on or just inside the line. Keep your scissors stationary and rotate the wool with your other hand to trim around the shapes so you don't bevel the edges.

Paper side of fusible web →

Wrong side of fabric →

From top to bottom: Watering Can (page 35); Sheep (page 53); and Coffee, Pray, Hustle (page 42)

6 Remove the paper backing from all of the appliqué shapes except the backing square. For each shape, hold the shape in your nondominant hand with the paper side up. Fold over a corner of the appliqué so that the paper touches paper. Press the folded corner between your fingers and make a motion as if you're snapping your fingers. This maneuver helps loosen the paper from the fusible adhered to the wool. Now you can pull off the paper.

7 Referring to the project photo and working from the bottom to the top, position the appliqués on the right side of the front square, leaving at least ⅛" on all sides for trimming later.

8 Once all the appliqués are in place, it's time to turn on the steam. Set your iron on the highest wool setting. Position the soleplate of the iron directly above the appliqués you're fusing and place it squarely on top of them. Using MAXIMUM STEAM and moving the iron up and down, fuse the layers together. Sometimes I do a quick prepress and check to make sure nothing has adhered to the iron (it happens). If it's all good, I repeat with additional pressure.

9 Referring to "Embroidery for Itty Bitties" on page 12, follow the project instructions to blanket stitch around each appliqué shape first, using size 12 pearl cotton or three strands of floss

in a matching color, unless otherwise indicated. Add any remaining stitching details as instructed, stitching in the order given and referring to the photo as needed.

10 If you're using Press'n Seal to transfer words or an embroidered design to the front square, position the traced design on the right side of the square and stitch through it using the stitch(es) indicated. Cut away the Press'n Seal as close as you can to the stitching, and then use tweezers to pull it out sideways from underneath the stitching.

11 Remove the fusible-web paper from the back square. Place the front and back squares wrong sides together. Fuse the squares together using lots of steam. Trim the piece to 2" to 2⅛" square, keeping the design centered. Using size 8 pearl cotton in a matching color, blanket stitch around the square, hiding the starts and stops between the square layers.

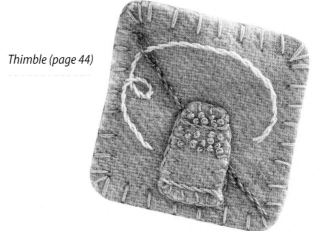

Thimble (page 44)

embroidery for itty bitties

Now for the fun part! I absolutely love using needle and thread to add personality and texture to these little projects. Even the functional blanket stitching around the shapes to hold them down adds interest.

Each project will list the stitch and thread color used for each detail, with the color number and thread size in parentheses. If floss is used, the number of strands will be specified. Thread colors are based on the wool colors I used, so use whatever works best for the wool colors you've chosen.

Use a length of thread approximately 18" long when working the stitches. Any longer than that and your thread will tangle and start to look scruffy after repeatedly pulling it through the fabric. Work the stitches in the order given for best results.

The illustrations in this section show how to make the stitches used for the projects. For more in-depth information and step-by-step photos for making each stitch, refer to my book *Wool, Needle & Thread*.

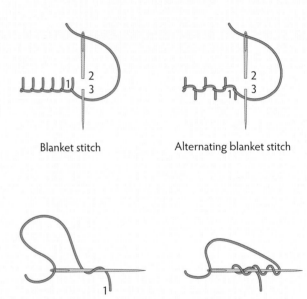

Blanket stitch

Alternating blanket stitch

Colonial knot

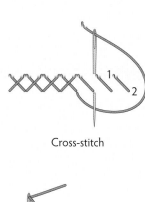

Cross-stitch

Fly stitch

Lazy daisy stitch

Double lazy
daisy stitch

Satin stitch

Stem stitch

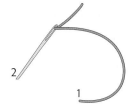

Straight stitch

*happy is the
new pretty*

+ **Words:** stem stitch
in Beaver Gray
(135, size 12)

HAPPY
is the
New
PRETTY

happy new year

+ **Happy:** stem stitch in Charcoal (2, size 12)
+ **New Year:** stem stitch in Mother Goose Medium (143, size 12)
+ **Stars:** straight stitch in Backyard Honeycomb (M81, size 12)

snowman

+ **Scarf:** stem stitch in Shimmering Denim (O561, size 8)
+ **Arms:** straight stitch in Brown Vintage Hues (P12, 3 strands floss)
+ **Nose:** satin stitch in Cinnamon Swirl (O506, size 12)
+ **Eyes and buttons:** colonial knot in Black Dyed (1, size 8)

snowflake

+ **Long lines through snowflake:** stem stitch in Light Ecru (5, size 8)
+ **Short lines:** straight stitch in Light Ecru (5, size 8)

mittens

+ **Cuffs:** blanket stitch wide stitches on edge of cuff and fill in with blanket stitches on opposite edge in Mother Goose Medium (143, size 12)
+ **Snowflakes:** straight stitch and colonial knots in Light Ecru (5, size 12)

groundhog

+ **Paws:** straight stitch in Mother Goose Medium (143, size 12)

+ **Top of nose:** satin stitch in Mother Goose Medium (143, size 12)

+ **Bottom of nose:** satin stitch in Muddy Bark (O196, size 12)

+ **Nose outline:** straight stitch in Black Dyed (1, size 12)

+ **Eyes:** colonial knot in Black Dyed (1, size 12)

+ **Ears:** double lazy daisy stitches in Muddy Bark (O196, size 12)

+ **Dirt clumps:** colonial knots in Muddy Bark (O196; size 12)

be mine

+ **Letters:** stem stitch in Black Dyed (1, size 12)

snowman love

+ **Buttons and eyes:** colonial knots in Black Dyed (1, size 12)
+ **Mouth:** straight stitch in Black Dyed (1, size 12)
+ **Nose:** satin stitch in Faded Rust Dark (863, size 12)
+ **Arms:** stem stitch in Muddy Bark (O196, size 8)
+ **String:** stem stitch in Pearl Gray (118, size 12)
+ **Hearts:** double lazy daisy stitches in Nostalgic Rose (H204, size 12), Turkey Red (O775, size 12), Raspberry (O522, size 12), Old Rose Light (841, size 12), and Distant Mauve Dark (883, size 12)
+ **Snow:** colonial knots in Light Ecru (5, size 12)

heart

+ **XO:** straight stitch in Black Dyed (1, size 12)

george and abe

shamrock

st. patrick's day

+ **Shamrock stem:** stem stitch in Green Pastures
  (O526, size 12)
+ **Buckle:** cross-stitch in Tarnished Gold
  (P5, size 12)

rabbit

+ **Eye:** colonial knot in Light Ecru (5, size 12)
+ **Stem and leaves:** stem stitch in Crispy Leaf (O575, size 5)
+ **Flower:** double lazy daisy stitches and colonial knots in Fuchsia Love (V3, size 12)

easter cross

+ **Sun:** alternating blanket stitch in Light Ecru (5, size 12)
+ **Cross:** cross-stitch in Muddy Bark (O196, size 12)
+ **Stems:** straight stitch in Green Olives (O519, size 12)
+ **Flower buds:** colonial knots in Light Ecru (5, size 12)

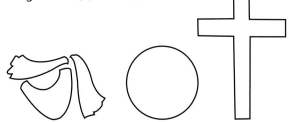

chick

+ **Wing:** stem stitch in Lemon (10, size 8)
+ **Eye:** colonial knot in Black Dyed (1, size 12)
+ **Beak:** satin stitch in Dark Antique Golds (O154, size 12)
+ **Feet:** straight stitch in Dark Antique Golds (O154, size 12)
+ **Bird seed:** colonial knots in Blurry Vanilla (M67, size 12)

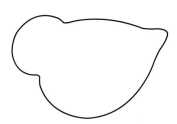

basketball

+ **Net:** stem stitch in Light Ecru (5, size 12)
+ **Rim and swoosh lines:** stem stitch in Chimney Dust (O512, size 12 doubled)
+ **Lines on ball:** stem stitch in Black Dyed (1, size 12)

gardening

+ **Bucket handle and rim:** stem stitch in Pearl Gray (118, size 12)
+ **Stems:** stem stitch in Green Olives (O519, size 12)
+ **Leaves:** lazy daisy stitch in Green Olives (O519, size 12)
+ **Blue flower:** lazy daisy stitch in Denim Light (M46, size 12)
+ **Flower center:** colonial knot in Backyard Honeycomb (M81, size 12)
+ **Purple flower:** colonial knots in Vintage Lavender (O542, size 12)
+ **Turquoise flower:** straight stitch in Bright Turquoise (93, size 12)

flowerpot

+ **Pot detail:** stem stitch in Light Ecru (5, size 12)
+ **Stems:** stem stitch in Rich Olive Green (190, size 12)

rainbow

+ **Rainbow:** stem stitch 2 rows of each color:
  Ripened Plum (O86, size 5), Dusty Blue (112,
  size 8 doubled), Stormy Sky (O120, size 5),
  Green Pastures (O526, size 8 doubled),
  Tarnished Gold (P5, size 5), Terra Cotta Twist
  (O510, size 5), Turkey Red (O775, size 8)

duck

+ **Umbrella details:** stem stitch in Aged White
  Light (P4, size 12)
+ **Duck wing:** stem stitch in Backyard
  Honeycomb (M81, 3 strands floss)
+ **Duck eye:** colonial knot in Red Brown Dark
  (1645, size 12)

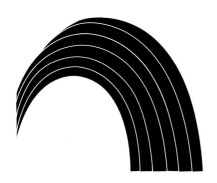

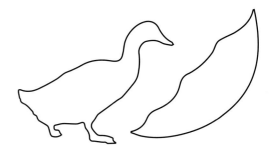

red-winged blackbird

+ **Beak and wing bottom:** satin stitch in Blurry Vanilla (M67, size 12)
+ **Wing top:** satin stitch in Turkey Red (O775, size 12)
+ **Bird's eye:** colonial knot in Red Brown Dark (1645, size 12)
+ **Branches:** cross-stitch in Muddy Bark (O196, size 12)

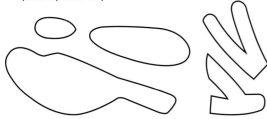

music

+ **Staff lines:** stem stitch in Black Dyed (1, size 12)
+ **Treble clef:** stem stitch in Black Dyed (1, size 8)
+ **Note heads:** stem stitch in Black Dyed (1, size 8)
+ **Note stems and flags:** straight stitch in Black Dyed (1, size 12)

folk-art flowers

+ **Flowers:** blanket stitch along top using long stitches in flower indentations and stem stitch curved edges in Light Ecru (5, size 12)

+ **Stems:** stem stitch in Light Medium Gray (122, size 8)

+ **Berries and center flower:** colonial knots in Light Ecru (5, size 12)

+ **Leaves:** double lazy daisy stitch in Light Medium Gray (122, size 8)

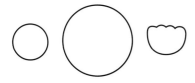

tulip

+ **Stem:** blanket stitch and then cross-stitch in Green Pastures (O526, 3 strands floss)

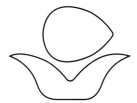

grow

+ **Grow:** stem stitch in Crispy Leaf (O575, size 8)
+ **Stem:** stem stitch in Crispy Leaf (O575, size 12)
+ **Leaves:** lazy daisy stitch in Crispy Leaf (O575, size 8)
+ **Large flower:** lazy daisy stitch in Blurry Vanilla (M67, size 12)
+ **Small flower:** lazy daisy stitch in Garnets (O503, size 12)
+ **Flower centers:** colonial knots in Red Brown Dark (1645, size 12)

beehive

+ **Beehive:** straight stitch in Dark Antique Golds (O154, 3 strands floss)
+ **Leaves:** lazy daisy stitch in Olive Green (P2, size 8)

birdhouse

- + **Roof and base:** cross-stitch in Black Dyed (1, size 8)
- + **Flowers:** lazy daisy stitch in Love of Life (O244, size 12)
- + **Flower centers:** colonial knots in Red Brown Dark (1645, size 12)
- + **Leaves:** lazy daisy stitch in Crispy Leaf (O575, size 8)

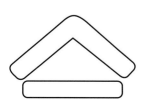 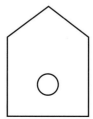

mason jar

Note: Finished size of Itty Bitty shown measures 2" × 2⅜". Cut your wool squares 2½" × 2½" and trim to size when complete.

- + **Stem:** stem stitch in Crispy Leaf (O575, size 8)
- + **Leaves:** lazy daisy stitch in Crispy Leaf (O575, size 8)
- + **Petals:** double lazy daisy stitch in Vintage Lavender (O542, size 12)
- + **Flower center:** colonial knot in Black Dyed (1, size 8)

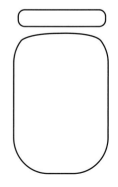

strawberries

+ **Calyx:** long blanket stitches worked from edge to center in Crispy Leaf (O575, size 12)
+ **Stems:** cross-stitch in Crispy Leaf (O575, size 12)
+ **Seeds:** straight stitch in Light Ecru (5, size 12)

tennis

+ **Ball detail:** stem stitch in Spring Greens (O19, 3 strands floss)
+ **Racket head:** cross-stitch in Light Ecru (5, size 12)
+ **Handle:** satin stitch in Beaver Gray (135, size 12)
+ **Strings:** straight stitch in over-and-under pattern in Mother Goose Medium (143, size 12)

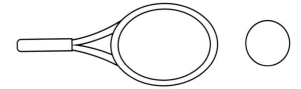

sun

bicycle

+ **Bicycle fenders:** stem stitch in Light Ecru (5, size 8)

+ **Bicycle frame, handles, seat, pedals, and tires:** stem stitch in Light Ecru (5, size 12)

+ **Wheel center:** colonial knot in Light Ecru (5, size 12)

+ **Chain wheel:** colonial knot in Light Ecru (5, size 8)

sand pail and shovel

+ **Shovel handle stem:** cross-stitch in Love of Life (O244, size 12)
+ **Top pail line:** stem stitch in Denim Light (M46, size 12)
+ **Middle pail lines:** stem stitch in Love of Life (O244, size 12)

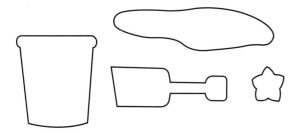

sailboat

+ **Stripes in sail and flag:** stem stitch in Turkey Red (O775, size 8)

flip-flops

+ **Straps:** cross-stitch in Old Cottage Grey (O126, size 12)
+ **Flowers:** lazy daisy stitch in Light Ecru (5, size 12)
+ **Flower centers:** colonial knot in Backyard Honeycomb (M81, size 12)

golf

+ **Flag pole:** stem stitch in Light Ecru (5, size 12)
+ **Number 1:** straight stitch in Turkey Red (O775, size 12)
+ **Golf ball:** colonial knot in Light Ecru (5, size 12)

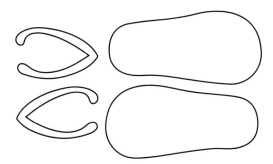

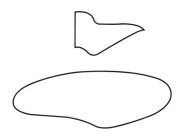

july 4th

+ **Words:** stem stitch in Black Dyed (1, size 12)

HAPPY
4TH OF JULY

baseball

+ **Stitching:** fly stitch in Turkey Red (O775, size 12)

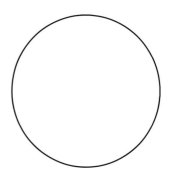

american flag

+ **Star:** straight stitch (3 times around inside) in Light Ecru (5, size 8)
+ **Stripes:** stem stitch in Turkey Red (O775, size 5)

lemonade

+ **Lemon slice details:** blanket stitch in Blurry Vanilla (M67, size 12)
+ **Lemon slice center:** colonial knot in Blurry Vanilla (M67, size 12)
+ **Jar:** stem stitch in Pearl Gray (118, size 12)

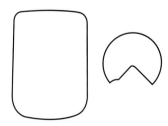

less monday

+ **Less & More:** stem stitch in Ivory (4, size 12)
+ **Monday & Summer:** stem stitch in Taupe Cream (222, size 12)

LESS
Monday
MORE
Summer

grape hyacinth

+ **Flowers:** colonial knots in Ripened Plum (O86, size 12) and Mauve Orchid (O541, size 12)
+ **Stems:** stem stitch in Crispy Leaf (O575, size 8)
+ **Veins in leaves:** stem stitch in Crispy Leaf (O575, size 12)

watering can

+ **Aqua flowers (not fused):** straight stitch between petals in Heavenly Hue (JP11, 3 strands floss)
+ **Aqua flower centers:** colonial knots in Backyard Honeycomb (M81, size 12)
+ **Light gray flowers:** double lazy daisy stitch in White Smoke Gray (117, size 12)
+ **Ends of light gray flowers:** straight stitch in Green Olives (O519, size 12)
+ **Leaves:** lazy daisy stitch in Green Olives (O519, size 12)

watermelon

+ **Inside rind:** cross-stitch in Olives (M19, size 12)
+ **Seeds:** lazy daisy stitch in Aged Black (P11, size 8)

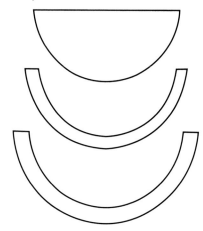

schoolhouse

+ **Ground and circle window:** chain stitch in Mother Goose Medium (143, size 12)
+ **Window panes:** straight stitch in Black Dyed (1, size 12)

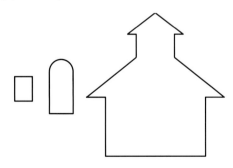

sunflower

+ **Sunflower center:** long blanket stitches worked from edge to center in Red Brown Dark (1645, size 12)
+ **Sunflower:** short-long blanket stitch in Backyard Honeycomb (M81, size 12)
+ **Stem:** cross-stitch in Crispy Leaf (O575, size 12)

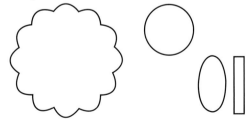

apple

+ **Stem:** stem stitch in Brown (P12, size 12)
+ **Highlight:** stem stitch in Spring Greens
  (O19, use 6 strands floss)

football

+ **Football details:** stem stitch in Ivory (4, size 12)

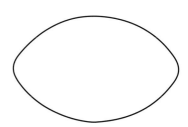

willow tree

+ **Tree branches:** stem stitch in Red Brown Dark
  (1645, size 12)
+ **Leaves:** lazy daisy stitch in Green Olives
  (O519, size 12)

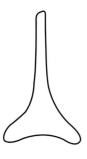

dragonfly

+ **Body:** blanket stitch in Black Nut (O531, size 8)
+ **Head and tail:** colonial knots in Black Nut
  (O531, size 8)

wine

+ **Wine bottle neck:** cross-stitch in Green Olives (O519, 3 strands floss)
+ **Cork:** straight stitch in Muddy Bark (O196, size 12)
+ **Glass:** stem stitch in Pearl Gray (118, size 12)
+ **Grape vine:** stem stitch in Crispy Leaf (O575, size 12)
+ **Wine:** stem stitch in Aged Wine (O78, size 12)
+ **Leaves:** double lazy daisy stitch in Crispy Leaf (O575, size 8)
+ **Grapes:** colonial knots in Mauve Orchid (O541, size 12)

more than chocolate

+ **Words:** stem stitch in Light Ecru (5, size 12)
+ **Heart:** stem stitch in Turkey Red (O775, size 5)

puppy

+ **Puppy details:** stem stitch in Mother Goose Medium (143, size 12)
+ **Nose:** satin stitch in Black Dyed (1, size 12)
+ **Eyes:** colonial knots in Black Dyed (1, size 12)

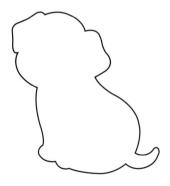

love

cat

+ **Leg details:** stem stitch in Pearl Gray (118, size 12)
+ **Whiskers:** straight stitch in Cottage Smoke (O538, 3 strands floss)
+ **Eyes:** straight stitch in Black Dyed (1, 3 strands floss)
+ **Nose:** satin stitch in Pearl Gray (118, size 8)
+ **Mouth:** straight stitch in Pearl Gray (118, size 12)

fish

+ **Fish detail:** stem stitch in Juniper Medium (892, size 12)
+ **Fish eye:** colonial knot in Juniper Medium (892, size 12)
+ **Line:** stem stitch in White Smoke Gray (117, size 12)
+ **Hook:** stem stitch in Mother Goose Medium (143, size 12)

coffee, pray, hustle

+ **Coffee & Hustle:** stem stitch in Aged White Light (P4, size 12)
+ **Pray:** stem stitch in Aged Black (P11, size 12)

heart of our home

+ **Roof:** cross-stitch in Light Ecru (5, size 12)

Coffee
PRAY
Hustle

home sweet home

+ **Words:** stem stitch in Subtle Elegance
  (M49, size 8)
+ **Heart:** lazy daisy stitch in Subtle Elegance
  (M49, size 8)

house

+ **Stem:** stem stitch in Olive Green (P2, size 12)
+ **Windows:** straight stitch in Black Dyed
  (1, size 12)

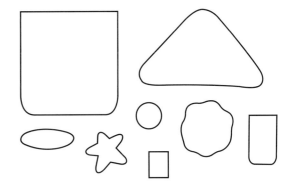

thimble

+ **Needle:** stem stitch in Chimney Dust (O512, size 12)
+ **Thread:** stem stitch in Light Ecru (5, size 12)
+ **Thimble lines:** stem stitch in Pearl Gray (118, size 12)
+ **Thimble indentations:** colonial knots in Pearl Gray (118, size 12)

scissors

+ **Scissors:** cross-stitch in Pearl Gray (118, 3 strands floss)
+ **Screw:** colonial knot in Pearl Gray (118, 3 strands floss)

sewing machine

+ **Spool:** satin stitch in Muddy Bark
  (O196, size 12)
+ **Needle and thread guide:** straight stitch in
  Mother Goose Medium (143, size 12)
+ **Thread:** satin stitch around spool, straight
  stitch to guide and needle in Pond Ripple
  (O544, 3 strands floss)

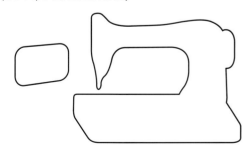

seam ripper

+ **Love & Hate:** stem stitch in Black Dyed
  (1, size 12)
+ **Relationship:** straight stitch in Black Dyed
  (1, size 12)
+ **Handle:** stem stitch in Muddy Bark
  (O196, size 12)
+ **Blade:** stem stitch
  in Pearl Gray
  (118, size 12)
+ **Ball:** colonial knot
  in Turkey Red
  (O775, size 12)

be kind

+ **Circle and words:** stem stitch in Black Dyed
  (1, size 12)
+ **Leaves:** lazy daisy stitch in Black Dyed
  (1, size 12)

star

+ **Star shape:** straight stitch in Black Dyed
  (1, size 12**)**

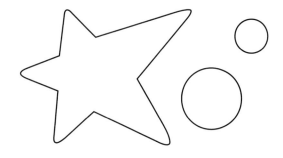

birthday cake

+ **Candles:** stem stitch one candle each in Tea Honey (O571, size 12), Deep Waters (M30, size 12), Turkey Red (O775, size 12), Green Olives (O519, size 12), Light Lilac (82, size 12), and Love of Life (O244, size 12)
+ **Flames:** lazy daisy stitch in Backyard Honeycomb (M81, size 12)

balloons

+ **Green balloon neck:** straight stitch in Explosion in Greens (M79, size 12)
+ **Yellow balloon neck:** straight stitch in Backyard Honeycomb (M81, size 12)
+ **Red balloon neck:** straight stitch in Turkey Red (O775, size 12)
+ **Blue balloon neck:** straight stitch in Denim Light (M46, size 12)
+ **Strings:** stem stitch in Beaver Gray (135, size 12)

book

+ **Book outlines:** stem stitch in Black Dyed
  (1, size 12)
+ **Designs on pages:** straight stitch in Black Dyed
  (1, size 12)

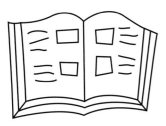

pincushion

+ **Pincushion details:** stem stitch in Old Brick
  (P1, size 12)
+ **Pin shafts:** straight stitch in Beaver Gray
  (135, size 12)
+ **Pin heads:** colonial knots in Beaver Gray
  (135, size 12)

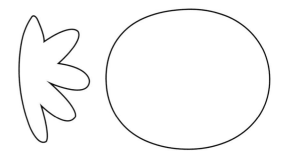

needle & thread

+ **Thread:** stem stitch in Light Ecru (5, size 12)
+ **Needle:** stem stitch in Mother Goose Medium (143, size 12)

hexagons

happy fall

+ **Happy & Fall:** stem stitch in Yummy Pumpkin
  (O217, size 12)
+ **Y'ALL:** stem stitch in Red Brown Dark
  (1645, size 12)

Happy
Fall
Y'ALL

pumpkin

+ **Pumpkin details:** stem stitch in Coffee Roast
  (O513, size 12)

harvest moon

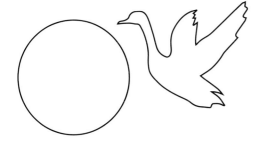

acorns

+ **Leaf veins:** fly stitch in Muddy Bark
  (O196, size 12)
+ **Acorn stems:** satin stitch in Muddy Bark
  (O196, size 12)

trick or treat

+ **Words:** stem stitch in Ivory (4, size 12)

TRICK
or
TREAT

ghost

+ **Eyes and mouth:** colonial knots in Black Dyed (1, size 8)

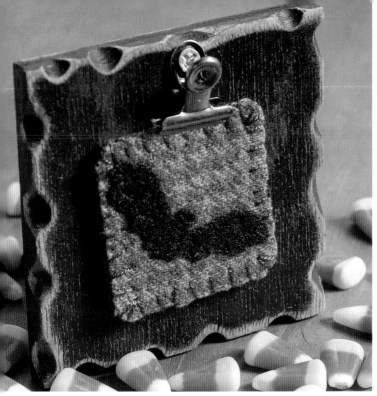

bat

sheep

+ **Body:** colonial knots in Aged White Light (P4, size 8)
+ **Eyes:** colonial knots in Faded Brown (H212, size 12)

maple leaf

+ **Stem:** cross-stitch in Brown (P12, size 12)
+ **Veins:** stem stitch in Brown (P12, size 12)

maple tree

give thanks ⌒

+ **Words:** stem stitch in Aged White Light (P4, size 8)

Give Thanks

turkey

+ **Buckle:** straight stitch in Tarnished Gold (P5, size 12)
+ **Beak:** satin stitch in Tarnished Gold (P5, size 12)
+ **Eyes:** colonial knots in Muddy Bark (O196, size 12)
+ **Heart:** double lazy daisy stitch in Turkey Red (O775, size 12)

hockey

+ **Stick toe:** blanket stitch in Subtle Elegance (M49, 3 strands floss)
+ **Stick shaft:** cross-stitch in Subtle Elegance (M49, 3 strands floss)
+ **Stick details:** satin stitch in Black Dyed (1, size 12)

ice skates

+ **Blades:** stem stitch in Chimney Dust (O512, size 12)
+ **Laces:** straight stitch and lazy daisy loops in Black Dyed (1, size 8)

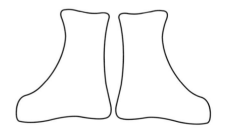

mountains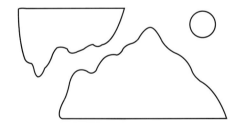

evergreens

pennies

hot chocolate

+ **Steam:** stem stitch in Pearl Gray (118, size 12)
+ **Snowflake:** lazy daisy stitch in Muddy Bark (O196, size 12)
+ **Snowflake ends:** straight stitch in Muddy Bark (O196, size 12)
+ **Marshmallows:** colonial knots in Light Ecru (5, size 12)

star of david

+ **Star:** straight stitch in Luminous Rich Navy (105, size 12)

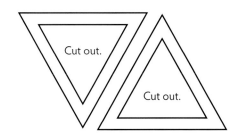

noel

+ **Noel:** stem stitch in Turkey Red (O775, size 12)
+ **Flower:** double lazy daisy stitch in Subtle Elegance (M49, size 8)
+ **Flower center:** colonial knots in Backyard Honeycomb (M81, size 12)

merry christmas

+ **Merry:** stem stitch in Crispy Leaf (O575, size 12)
+ **Christmas:** stem stitch in Turkey Red (O775, size 12)
+ **Tree:** satin stitch in Crispy Leaf (O575, size 12)

christmas candle

+ **Pine needles:** fly stitch in Crispy Leaf (O575, size 12)
+ **Berries:** colonial knots in Turkey Red (O775, size 12)

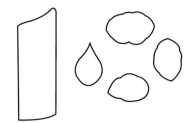

christmas bell

+ **Bell stripe:** stem stitch in Turkey Red (O775, size 12)
+ **Berries:** colonial knots in Turkey Red (O775, size 12)
+ **Holly leaf veins:** stem stitch in Blackened Khaki Brown (O548, 3 strands floss)

poinsettia

+ **Veins:** straight stitch in Crispy Leaf (O575, 3 strands floss)
+ **Centers:** colonial knots in Backyard Honeycomb (M81, size 12)

santa

+ **Hat trim:** cross-stitch in Light Ecru (5, size 8)
+ **Pom-pom:** straight stitch in Light Ecru (5, size 12)
+ **Eyebrows and nose:** straight stitch in Muddy Pots (JP6, size 12)
+ **Eyes:** colonial knots in Shimmering Denim (O561, size 12)

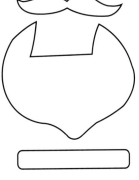

candy canes

+ **Stripes:** straight stitch in Turkey Red (O775, size 8)
+ **Veins:** stem stitch in Crispy Leaf (O575, size 12)
+ **Berries:** colonial knots in Turkey Red (O775, size 8)

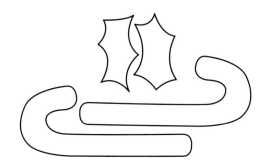

reindeer

+ **Antlers:** straight stitch in Brown (P12, 2 strands floss)
+ **Eyes:** colonial knots in Black Dyed (1, size 8)
+ **Nose:** satin stitch in Black Dyed (1, size 8)
+ **Snowflake:** straight stitch and colonial knots in Aged White Light (P4, size 8)

martini time

+ **Glass outline:** stem stitch in Pearl Gray (118, size 12)
+ **Glass details:** stem stitch in Santa Fe (M44, size 12)
+ **Drink:** satin stitch in Aged White Light (P4, size 8)
+ **Cocktail pick:** straight stitch in Muddy Bark (O196, size 12)
+ **Pimento:** French knot in Turkey Red (O775, size 8)

about the author

You can't be around designer Lisa Bongean for long without picking up her infectious enthusiasm for stitching, both by hand and by machine. But if pressed, she'll probably tell you her heart is with wool stitchery. The combination of richly textured wools, delightfully colorful threads, and the endless array of shapes that you can cut—she's a fan of it all! Which is probably why she's been a teacher to so many stitchers over the years. There's little that she hasn't tried, and so much that she's learned and is willing to share. She's matter-of-fact about the tools and supplies she likes to use and why. If practice, practice, practice is the key to getting it right, it's clear that's why Lisa Bongean's a leader in the wool stitchery world. Her workmanship is impeccable because she never stops making more.

The owner of Primitive Gatherings (PrimitiveGatherings.us), Lisa has shops in both Menasha, Wisconsin, and Murrieta, California, that specialize in hand-dyed wools, quilting cottons, and kits.